BASIL'S DEAL

Pictures from Basil Kidd's photographic archive

by Judith Gaunt

Bygone Publishing

A catalogue record for this book is available from the British Library

ISBN 978-0-9566172-0-0

Printed and bound in Great Britain by Geerings Print, Ashford, Kent

Also by Judith Gaunt: Shops Remembered in Deal and Walmer

Front cover photographs:
Royal Marines drilling on Deal seafront
Thelma Davies hangs out rugby team shirts
Princess Diana meets the crowds in Deal

Back cover photograph:
Actor Richard Hearne, alias Mr Pastry, meets
members of Walmer lifeboat crew

CONTENTS

DEDICATION

To Nick Kidd with my grateful thanks for his generosity.

INTRODUCTION

My first hazy memory of Basil was as photographer at my sister's wedding in 1970. I remember the embarrassment of being bridesmaid and the unexpected cold snow of March numbing my feet through light pumps as we stood for photographs outside St Leonard's Church at Upper Deal. I recall Basil's diplomacy at dealing with family politics and – of course like everyone else who was photographed by him – I remember the raspberry.

We next met in 1971 when I joined the East Kent Mercury as a cub reporter and there followed nearly six years of visits with Basil to fetes, annual dinners and the wealth of other local events that are the stuff of local journalism and pictures that sell papers. I remember one early morning job when, to my concern and confusion, he turned the car into the Royal Marines' barracks on our way to another job. "Wait here Jude," said Basil as he nipped out and quickly photographed a group of Marines, lined up ready and waiting for him.

Later in life if I went to a local event Basil would arrive, several cameras strung round his neck, a cheery wave, call of 'Hi, Jude', and a raspberry to the many people who would greet him fondly. A hand through his hair, to push away the curls, then a hand in his pocket to find a scrap of paper for notes. "A whisky Basil?" someone would ask and then he was off – to the next event.

On Monday mornings Basil would arrive at the East Kent Mercury office, the kettle would be on and he would remind the staff he had worked all weekend and been up all Sunday night while they slept, developing the prints for the Editor to choose from first thing on Monday. Out would come the fist full of crumpled scraps of paper and the occasional reporter notebooks. "I have to buy mine, not like you lot," and amazingly, virtually every time, the right information would connect with the appropriate photograph.

So many people have their own anecdotes and memories of Basil. Never did I think mine would begin the introduction to a book of his photographs. Time and again I have thanked Basil's son Nick, for the flattering, generous honour of being offered Basil's archive of photographs for use in a book. 'But you should do it,' said Nick in that no nonsense tone of Basil, with the same sense of generosity and buzz. Thank you Nick and thanks Basil. I hope I have done you both proud.

Judith Gaunt
Deal
October 2010

BASIL'S EARLY LIFE

Basil Michael Kidd was born on 11th March 1923 in Water Street, Deal, and attended the Wesleyan School in Union Road, also known as the Methodist School and now Wesleyan House. Basil was a choirboy at the Royal Marines Church of St Michael and All Angels in Canada Road, Walmer, and described himself as 'one of the angels.'

In 1937 Basil joined the Royal Marines, then called the Royal Navy School of Music, at Walmer, and was taught to play the oboe.

When the Second World War was declared Basil served on four Royal Navy cruisers – HMS Devonshire, Norfolk, London and Kent – and on the staff of the Rear Admiral 1st Cruiser Squadron. Most of that time was spent on the notorious and gruelling Russia bound Arctic convoys, where Basil was either in an eight inch gun turret as range finder or in a transmitting station.

Basil later recorded in a notebook of his memories that when the band did play on these missions, the instruments sometimes froze. Another problem was that reeds for the oboes were unobtainable as the cane for them came from France.

One of Basil's most memorable actions was taking part in the sinking of the German battleship Bismarck in May 1941 while a teenager aboard HMS Norfolk. In the summer of the following year, Basil sailed on the controversial convoy PQ17, a group of 35 ships which ran the German gauntlet. Only 11 vessels eventually reached the Soviets. In all 153 lives were lost along with 3,350 military vehicles, 430 tanks, 210 bombers and other vital supplies. For this, he was awarded the Russian Convoy Medal by Premier Mikhail Gorbachev – 50 years after the event.

It was on his first ship that the Rear Admiral detailed Basil to take photographs, a task he enjoyed and continued to do. 'Can't imagine doing anything else,' he later wrote in his notes. After the war he joined the Central Mediterranean Band, mainly based in Malta.

In 1953 Basil left the Royal Marines and briefly became Photographic Manager of the cruise liner New York making crossings from Southampton to New York. But in around 1954 he returned to Deal, first to Franklin's photographers in Victoria Road, then turning freelance from his home for many years at 32 Victoria Road.

Basil Kidd, with trusty
Nikon around his neck,
sometime in the 1970s.

PIER AND SEAFRONT

1 A dramatic shot by Basil Kidd of the RAF's Red Arrows aerobatic display team flying low over Deal during one of their visits for the Deal Regatta celebrations in the early 1970s. It was a time when there was still a good number of working fishermen and fishing boats moored on the beach.

2 Another view of the Red Arrows, their Gnat jets skilfully balanced in the photograph with the seaward end of Deal pier beneath – not an easy task given the speed at which the team flies. The photograph shows the Goodwin's Bar and Café, the flat roofed and tiled wall building popular with locals and visitors for cups of tea and 'a full English' breakfast. Sadly the café was demolished in 2009 and replaced with a timber framed and roofed construction.

3 Crowds await the arrival of the Duke of Edinburgh at the opening of Deal pier
on 19th November 1957. Prince Phillip can be seen approaching on the left,
followed by columns of Royal Marines. Local schoolchildren, Girl Guides
and Brownies line the route on the seaward side. Basil and other
photographers stood on the roof of the original Quarterdeck
building to take the pictures. The scene captures the Victorian
shelter on the promenade which was later replaced.

4 Prince Phillip, accompanied by the Mayor of Deal, Sidney Stewart Dunn, smiles at waiting schoolchildren and local people as he approaches the new Deal pier to perform the opening ceremony on 19th November 1957. A naval photographer records the occasion, a job Basil had done in his former life as a Royal Marine bandsman, having been detailed by his Admiral to take photographs on board ship – his introduction to photography.

When Basil left the Royal Marines he took a job as a cruise ship photographic manager travelling between Southampton and New York but he returned to Deal around 1954 and began his career as a local photographer. Towards the left of the shot, holding a notepad and pen, is a young Tony Arnold later to become chief reporter on the East Kent Mercury and colleague of Basil's.

5 Prince Philip stands at the entrance to the new pier to perform the opening ceremony, watched by Mayor of Deal, Sidney Stewart Dunn, local dignitaries and officials. Many of the women guests are wearing hats and, less contentious then, fur coats.

The previous pier had been damaged beyond repair on 29th January 1940, when the 350 ton Dutch cargo ship 'Nora' crashed into it after being bombed while anchoring in the Downs. In 1943 the Government finally agreed to pay compensation towards a new pier. Plans for the design were approved in 1954 and a tender of £218,441 accepted from Concrete Piling Ltd.

6 The breadth of Basil Kidd's career as a local photographer is underlined in this and the next photograph. Here the steamer the 'Queen of the Channel' approaches the newly built Deal pier, possibly at the end of July 1957, when the vessel called at the pierhead for the first time to take a party of 800 on a day's outing to Calais.

This view captures a glimpse of the lower, third deck, of the pier that is only seen at low tide. Miscalculations in the pier design and poor understanding of the tidal waters meant the third deck has never been in use as it is inaccessible.

7 Here is a more modern picture of a ship at the Deal pierhead taken two decades after the previous photograph. Young passengers are waiting to board a paddle steamer, possibly the 'Waverley', and likely to be one of the evening channel trips and disco the company ran for a while. There have periodically been attempts to revive the summer sailings from Deal, a popular idea given the queues in this picture.

8 A view of the beach showing the real working area of the Deal fishermen, with their winches, tool chests and other equipment of their trade. The picture is taken just south of The Royal Hotel, at the top of King Street. The photograph also shows the Victorian shelter that was sadly replaced by a new structure. The modern concrete sea defences had yet to be built in this view.

9 'I caught this one mister.' Children hold up their catches or carry them in plastic bags and gather round for a photocall at the end of a fishing competition on Deal pier. Duffle coats, plimsolls, sandals and home knitted jumpers date the photograph to the early 1960s. The Foc'sle fishing tackle shop, which was opposite the pier and sadly closed in 2007, is recorded on the fishing bags the boys are holding.

In the background, Deal's famous view back to the shoreline captures the many fishing boats that used to be kept on the foreshore, especially north of the pier.

10 Paul Amos is pictured with the 1,200lb and 12 feet long basking shark that he brought ashore at Deal on Saturday 5th November 1984. Paul and a colleague had gone out in the boat, owned by their boss who was away on honeymoon. They were fishing for bass off Sandwich Bay when the shark became caught in their driftnet.

The shark was nearly half the length of the boat and they couldn't land it so after a huge struggle they towed the shark back to shore. A few fishermen were needed to haul the shark into a van and it was taken down to the yard of Griggs fishmongers in South Street, where Basil took this picture, and from there on to Billingsgate Market, London, where it was sold.

Paul said afterwards they did not know when they were trying to land the beast that it did not have teeth.

11 Below, four year old Darryl Card struggles to hold the 17lb cod that is nearly as tall as he is. Darryl caught the cod in January 1974 while fishing off Deal beach with his dad Jim, who naturally had to help him land the fish.

12 Above, JW Pevy with his catch of a 38lb ling.

13 Bill Peacock with the 42lb conger eel that he caught at Deal.

14 Middle Street car park is pictured during the weigh in of a Southern Television fishing competition. Seated on the extreme left is Jack Hargreaves, presenter of the channel's Out of Town programme. Alongside him is Alderman Alistair Lawton who was Mayor of Deal in 1966 and 1967.

In the background is the rear of the High Street shops including an advertising sign on the outbuilding of Harris Mayes the butchers of 44 High Street, now Clark's shoes. The outbuilding, other premises and houses were demolished to create the Middle Street car park after the area was badly bombed during the Second World War.

15 Deal seafront photographed as fondly remembered by most Dealites and
visitors – a bustling hive of activity with dozens of fishing boats and fishermen.
Crowds gather around the day's catch and others stroll past the Regent
bingo hall, formerly the Regent cinema. On the right, in the distance,
the Queen's Hotel still stands before fire ravaged it in April 1981
and on the left a parade of beach huts, all long gone.

16 Eyes down. The Regent bingo club, a landmark of Deal seafront in its heyday, pictured with a game in session. Sadly the club closed for good in 2009, the smoking ban, taxes and online bingo given as the reasons.

Managing Director and owner Robin Bloom, who had run the Regent since 1965, told the East Kent Mercury: "A lot of our customers enjoy a cigarette so many have stopped coming. So heavy is the taxation on bingo, while we will be losing between £100,000 and £150,000 each year, the Government will actually make between £250,000 and £300,000 in taxes."

Earlier, the premises had been the Regent cinema but had been built in 1929 as the Pavilion for local entertainments. In June 2010 Dover District Council sold the freehold to Silver Screen Cinemas so the building may yet once again be a local cinema.

STORMS, SNOW AND FLOODS

17 Deal seafront, at the top of South Street, shows the full force the sea and weather can throw at the coastline during storms. In January 1978, when Basil took this photograph, dozens of boats were still moored here with the gear and equipment of the working fishermen. The weather had no mercy for any of it, throwing boats, shingle and debris up and over the road.

18 Fishermen and locals check on the damage to boats and equipment after violent storms in January 1978. They stand on the roadway, shingle beneath their feet and road signs for once unnecessary on the blocked road.

19 Another view of the storm damage on Deal seafront in January 1978 takes in a closer view of the former Regent bingo hall, its poster proclaiming 'Cash bingo. Prize bingo daily.'

20 The flooding at the bottom of South Street on 12th January 1978 ignored the
No Entry and temporary signs at the foot of the posts saying 'One way flow of
traffic.' A special Mercury supplement contained many photos taken by Basil of
the flooding which was descibed as the worst in the town for 25 years.
Damage estimated £1.5 million was caused in less than two hours.

21 'Top her up,' Basil has written on the back of this photograph of Ebden's Garage staff in Gilford Road making the most of a bad situation during summer flooding on 5 August 1979. In the canoe are Tony Cole, front, and Pat McDonagh while standing ready to serve the petrol is John Phoenix.

22 This photo of the 1978 flooding along Victoria Road and Basil's picture
records not only the bemused motorist and passenger in their Mk III
Ford Cortina but also the businesses of the time including Courts
furniture store, Dalton's estate agents and the Coffee Inn.

23 Deal seafront, along Prince of Wales Terrace, looking picturesque with its covering of snow. Once again the picture has recorded the boats and equipment of the working fishermen which were all along the seafront at one time.

24 A Deal Borough Council Bedford lorry, with a snow plough on the front, clears a way along Station Road, Walmer, at the approach to Dover Road; opposite is the Esso petrol sign for the Green Garage. The picture was taken in 1969 when, unlike now, the council had depots in West Street and Western Road with vehicles, equipment, piles of grit and a workforce of more than two dozen on hand to tackle snow clearance.

Tony Cheeseman, former superintendent of Highways and Cleansing, recalled he and his men worked day and night in exceptionally heavy snow. They were rewarded with letters of thanks from the Mayor John Blake and Alderman Albert Cavell as well as a thank you party.

25 Basil's photograph taken during heavy snow in February 1969 captures businesses that have long since closed. The view is taken on the Dover Road at the turning with Hawksdown Road. In the foreground are the traditional glass globe topped Shell petrol pumps of Hawksdown Garage. To the right is the edge of Thompson's Walmer Brewery which was demolished and replaced with housing.

26 Elizabeth Maltrap stands outside her home in Channel Lea, off Walmer Castle Road, on the morning of 17th October 1987 surveying the damage to her property from the hurricane that devastated large parts of Kent.

Mrs Maltrap had been indoors with her two young children when a pair of birch trees crashed through the roof of her house. As she rang the emergency services two more trees fell on to the property and Mrs Maltrap later said that she and the children were lucky to escape with their lives.

27 Traffic struggles on the Dover to Deal road in January 1966 when two people died
and hundreds were stranded during severe snowstorms and blizzard conditions.
On the left a lorry belonging to Alfred Olby Limited, builders' merchants
of Thanet, attempts to turn while another vehicle is abandoned.
The Ripple and Sutton traffic sign just stays above
snow level alongside The Mill Garage.

28 'A Bridge Too Far' was Basil's note written on the back of this photograph taken at the Hamilton Road and Telegraph Road junction in the late 1970s and shows PC Don Diprose on traffic duty with the unfortunate lorry driver alongside. This was just one of the occasions Basil photographed vehicles damaging the bridge.

In 1975 another lorry became stuck when the Queen was due to drive along Hamilton Road following a visit to Connaught Barracks in Dover. In the event her car was diverted along Gladstone Road.

29 It was a double-decker when it left the garage! Yet another collision with the bridge at Hamilton Road gives East Kent an unexpected addition to its fleet of open toppers! For bus enthusiasts, the vehicle was a 1967 registered AEC Regent with Park Royal body and is seen here sometime in the late 1970s wearing the poppy red livery of the National Bus Company, of which East Kent was a subsidiary.

WALMER LIFEBOAT AND THE GOODWIN SANDS

30 The crew of the Walmer lifeboat 'Charles Dibdin' and owner of the 36 feet cabin cruiser 'Sea Girl' watch helplessly as the boat burns. William Whitehouse and his son Charles had been on their way from Dover to Lowestoft when the boat caught fire off Kingsdown on 3rd June 1971. They were rescued by Brian Libby on his boat 'Cornishman' and transferred to the lifeboat under the charge of coxwain Harry Brown.

31 Head launcher, Les Coe, who celebrated 55 years service with Walmer lifeboat in 2010, watches as Lady Rose knocks the final pin from the slip chain of the 'Hampshire Rose' after performing the naming ceremony on 6 September 1975.

Lady Rose, wife of round the world yachtsman Sir Alec Rose, named the vessel on behalf of the people of Hampshire who raised the £95,000 for the craft that replaced the 'Charles Dibdin'.

'Hampshire Rose' was the last of the traditionally designed lifeboats and remained at Walmer until 1990 when it was replaced by the Atlantic 21 inshore craft the 'James Burgess'.

32 The 'Hampshire Rose' during the visit of the Duke of Kent on 1st May 1977
when the new inshore lifeboat was dedicated. Standing at the stern are, from left,
an unnamed RNLI official, Cyril Williams, the Duke of Kent, RNLI inspector Mr
Pennell, Coxwain Bruce Brown, lifeboat doctor Dr Alan Calder with crewmen
Brian Clark and Richard Chapman.

33 A dramatic shot of an RAF Air Sea Rescue helicopter as it hovers over 'Hampshire Rose', during a training exercise.

34 Crowds assembled for BBC's Songs of Praise on Walmer Green, broadcast on
Sunday 1st September 1974. To the left, behind the cameraman, are Mayor and
Mayoress of Deal Cllr Stuart and Mrs Doris Spears; Chairman of Dover District
Council Albert Cavell and Mrs Cavell, local choirs and schoolchildren, including
girls from St Ethelburga's Convent School in their traditional boaters. Further
along is a group of WRENS in their white hats, to the right of them the lifeboat
crew stands in front of the 'Charles Dibdin'. More local schoolchildren stand
before the band of the Royal Marines under the baton of Director
of Music Lt Col Paul Neville OBE MVO LRAM.

35-40 In this sequence of shots crew and helpers struggle to bring the 'Hampshire Rose' back ashore during a north easterly force eight gale. The lifeboat had been launched following a report to the coastguards saying a yacht had capsized. In the event, the crew of the yacht had actually taken down its sail and the lifeboat was not needed.

41 'Hampshire Rose' slips down the gangway for the last time on 6th May 1990 on her way to retirement. Crowds turned out for the occasion, boats and yachts lay waiting off shore and the RAF air sea rescue helicopter hovered overhead to say goodbye. 'Hampshire Rose' had completed 16 years service at Walmer and ended the history of traditional lifeboats at the station.

42 The Mayor of Deal, Cllr Alec Greenway-Stanley, presents a Certificate on Vellum to Bruce Brown, coxwain of the 'Hampshire Rose', and certificates to the crew in 1978. The awards were given for the crew's rescue of a husband, wife and their two children from the cabin cruiser 'Shark'. Bruce Brown later received the RNLI Bronze Medal at the Festival Hall in London for rescuing Cyril Williams, second coxwain during the incident.

Cyril's leg had become trapped in the cabin of the 'Shark' as he attempted to stem a leak after going aboard to fasten a towrope to the cruiser. Bruce, having pulled the semi-conscious Cyril free, momentarily passed out due to the exertion, but got them both clear just before the cruiser sank. Left to right receiving their awards are: Richard Ebden, David Steytler, Pat Hardman, Bruce Brown, Mayor of Deal Alec Greenway-Stanley, Cyril Williams, Dennis Brophy and Brian Clark.

43 Tug boats are dwarfed by the Liberian oil tanker 'Panther' as they attempt to pull it from the Goodwin Sands in April 1971 where it had been stuck for six days. The 15,841 ton tanker had 25,000 tons of crude oil on board and 2,000 tons were pumped out before the tanker could be towed off the Sands. Walmer lifeboat crews put to sea seven times during the incident.

Peter Rees, MP for Deal and Dover, who was also Trade and Industry Secretary toured the site. Kent Fire Brigade sprayed the beaches from North Deal to St Margaret's Bay in an attempt to disperse the oil slicks. Following the incident Parliament passed the Prevention of Oil Pollution Act 1971 giving it power to seize vessels if there was a threat of pollution.

44 'Kiddies Beware,' shouted the East Kent Mercury front page headline of 20th May 1971 which included this photograph by Basil. The caption began 'What's mummy going to say?' Four year old David Love (right) of Canada Road, Walmer, and three and a half year old Colin Ensore of Coppin Street, are covered in oil from the slick created by the 'Panther' after it ran aground on the Goodwin Sands.

45 George Pawson MBE, Auxiliary Coastguard District Officer since 1956,
was presented with gifts on his retirement in 1968 after 31 years service.
South East Inspector, Cmdr W Thomas, made the presentations at
Deal Rowing Club. To his left was Senior Station Officer, Nick Carter.

Among other Coastguards, RNLI and Rowing Club guests pictured were Henry
Stone, Joe (Jock) Milne, Cyril Swales, John Dunn, Alan Kirkaldie, Ray Sipek,
Alex Marsh, Dick Richards, Perce Cavell, Arthur Hobbs and Harry Brown.

In 1966 Mr Pawson had been selected from the National Auxiliary
Coastguard Service to go to Pearl Harbour to demonstrate
a new style rocket to the American Navy.

46 An unusual starting line for members of Deal Striders as they prepare for a race around the Goodwin Sands on 23rd June 1994. The runners were taking part in the second annual Julie Rose Memorial Race in memory of their late coach Cliff Temple, who supported the memorial fund.

47 Going off course had more than the usual repercussions so the race marshals
made sure they kept the Deal Striders firmly on track at
the Goodwin Sands on 23rd June 1994.

48 Solley's Farms Real Dairy Ice cream, Mongeham, have outlets throughout the
area – including the Goodwin Sands. David and Stephen Solley serve ice
cream from one of their carts during the trip to the Goodwin Sands. The
hovercraft, 'Princess Margaret', made the journey to the Sands taking
the Deal Striders and many day-trippers who enjoyed picnics,
games of boules, metal detecting and other activities.

49 In the 1970s a group of sailors working on three survey ships, which can just be seen in the background, decided to have a game of cricket on the Goodwin Sands. The paper top hats worn by the sailors recreated a match held on the Sands in 1919 when the players actually wore top hats.

Annual games of cricket were held on the sands until 2003 when they were banned for safety reasons. In 2006 a team from the BBC programme 'Coast' decided to recreate the tradition – only to be rescued by Ramsgate inshore lifeboat as the water quickly rose around them.

THE QUEEN'S HOTEL FIRE

ROTARY CLUB OF DEAL

40th ANNIVERSARY — 20th NOVEMBER, 1963

BASIL M. KIDD, Deal

Rtn. Bernard J. Kimpton   Rtn. Peter M. Hill   Rtn. Donald A. Bailiff   Rtn. Wilfred J. Barber   P.P. Vivyan K. Phillips   Rtn. Edward I. Rayner   P.P. Max J. Elfick
P.P. Albert E. M. Cavell   P.P. Bernard F. Bright   Rtn. W. James Fisk   P.P. Frank T. Colegrave   P.P. Reginald A. Sharp   Rtn. Cecil W. L. Prime
Rtn. John D. Daniell   P.P. F. Guy Farrant   P.P. Bert C. Dredge   Rtn. J. Clifford Jackson   Vice-President R. John Barnes   Rtn. Gilbert W. Langstaff   Rtn. Fred E. Farrier
Rtn. Eric L. Hartley   Rtn. Colin A. Joyce   Rtn. Walter W. Irwin   P.P. Frank W. B. Corcoran   P.P.S. Stewart Dunn   Rtn. Charles S. Smith   P.P. John W. Belfield
Rtn. Alfred G. N. Pope   Rtn. Charles Lock   Rtn. Julius W. Summerhayes   P.P. George A. Lawford   Rtn. F. Stanley Townend   Rtn. Roy R. Rudland
P.P. Reginald V. Jones   President Rev. Raymond W. Heath   Vice-President Peter J. Marriott   Rtn. Edward Gargett   P.P. Jack Parkin   Rtn. Basil M. Kidd   Rtn. S. Lawrence Cookman
Honorary Members : W. Eric Rice   Norman Cavell

50 A seemingly ordinary photo captured on the steps of the once majestic
Queen's Hotel celebrating the 40th anniversary of the Rotary Club in 1963.
Basil Kidd took the photograph but look closely and he had set up the shot
so that he could dash to his place second from the right of the front row.

51 Flames rise up through the roof of the imposing Queen's Hotel, which was gutted by fire on 9th April 1981. In his notebook recording his years as a photographer Basil wrote of the event: "Sat on beach all night. More flames — more water!"

The hotel was built as the South Eastern Hotel to cater for the growth of holiday visitors to the seaside. The site now houses The Queen's Mews apartment block.

52 Firemen on turntable ladders attempt to put out the flames. Fire engines from across east Kent were called to fight the fire.

53 Basil must have been on a firemen's turntable ladder to take this rooftop photo of the façade of The Queen's Hotel. Wallpaper can just be seen on one of the internal walls.

54 A fireman stands on the roof of The Queen's Hotel surrounded by tiles and debris.

55 Daylight and the full horror of The Queen's Hotel fire is revealed from the
side of the building in Ranelagh Road.

56 The cellar bar of The Queen's Hotel known as 'The Dive Bar' lies gutted as firemen survey the damage. The old till, glasses and sherry cask still sit on the shelves behind the bar.

57 Firemen inspect the charred and blackened inside of The Queen's Hotel.

58 Basil's dramatic shot, that looks to have been taken from the Deal Castle Road side of the building, shows the scale of the Queen's Hotel and the height the firemen had to reach on their turntable ladders.

59 The Queen's Hotel dining room in happier and grander times set out for the
staff Christmas party of Riceman's department store. Standing centre on the
top table is Fred Riceman, owner of the firm, and to his left his young
daughter Elizabeth and wife Betty. Behind the group can be
seen the French windows which led to the glass fronted balconies.

DEAL AND WALMER CIVIC LIFE

60 Deal Town Hall looking rather different than today as Deal Borough Council workmen remove the old doors that were in place when the under-croft was used for the town's fire engines. A Deal Borough Council barrow, familiar in its day, stands on the pavement.

61 The rear of Deal Town Hall photographed in 1962 after two houses had been demolished and the space used as a car park. The work exposed views usually hidden, including the Mayor's Parlour and some of the old cells of the former police station. The Borough of Deal notice board displays an Accident Prevention Committee safety notice. A glimpse of Castle's wine merchants can just be seen in the background on the corner of Oak Street and High Street, previously Nethersole's wine merchants.

62 Deal Borough Council sits in session for the Mayor making ceremony of Alderman Norman Cavell in May 1962. Ald Cavell, who created a precedent by choosing a woman as his deputy, Cllr Miss E Macrae, chose as his priorities for the year, the future of Betteshanger Colliery, re-planning of Middle Street and the difficulties faced by local boatmen.

To the extreme left is Ald EH Hopkinson, retiring Mayor, Ald John Tapping, and Ald JG Tooms. To the Mayor's right are Ald Ernest Cavell attending his 42nd Mayor making, Ald Albert Cavell and Ald Albert Jenkins. In the foreground at the centre table is the Town Clerk, Edgar Bradbury. Town Sergeant, Jock Cowie, stands guard in the doorway.

Members of the public are seated on the left and in the gallery, from where Basil took this photograph.

63 Aikman Duncan Cowie, was Town Sergeant of Deal from 1960 to 1984 and better known to all as "Jock" Cowie. Jock was born in Glasgow in 1922 and joined the Royal Artillery Parachute Regiment. During the Second World War Jock fought as a Commando and in May 1941, when the Germans invaded Crete, he was one of those who fought the rearguard action ordered by General Wavell, was captured and spent the rest of the war as a prisoner.

Jock married Betty in 1946 and had four children. The Town Sergeant's uniform he is wearing has not changed since its design in 1699 when Deal was granted its Charter by William III.

Joshua Coppin, the first Mayor of Deal, commissioned the mace carried by the Town Sergeant.

64 A service in St George's Church, Deal. Basil captured the quiet atmosphere in his photograph taken from the west gallery. To the left, in the north gallery are Deal Council members including the Mayor of 1966 and 1967 Ald Alistair Lawton while behind are members of the local constabulary.

In his History of Deal John Laker wrote of St George's Church: "In 1717 a gallery was erected on the north side of the chapel at a cost of £60, and the front seat of this gallery the corporation appropriated to itself as its official pew and has ever since retained possession of it."

On 7th November 2008 Basil's memorial service was held in St George's Church.

65 Town Sergeant Jock Cowie bows his head against snowfall as he leads Mayor Ald John Blake, councillors and officials into St Leonard's Church, Upper Deal, on Sunday 16th February 1969, the year of heavy snowfall. Ald Blake was Mayor of Deal in 1968 and 1969, and is followed by newly appointed Town Clerk, Ron Purnell.

At the church door to greet them is Rector John Gore and patiently standing in the snow are boys and a master from Tormore Preparatory School who attended service every Sunday. In the background is the former rectory.

66 'Bon Voyage' says the sign on a pillar inside St Leonard's Hall, Upper Deal, on the departure of Vicar of St Leonard's Church, Rev Colin Tufton, on 9th April 1967. Bill Sholl, Churchwarden, makes the presentation while right is John Hopper, People's Warden, and Rev Derek Atkinson, Curate and Priest in Charge of St Richard's Church.

67 Jock Cowie, Town Sergeant, leads the Mayor, Ald Norman Cavell, and Deal councillors from a service at St Mary's Church, Walmer, the route lined by schoolchildren and local Brownies, Guides and Scouts. Behind him are Ald Albert Cavell and Ald John Tapping, both former Mayors of the town.

68 Rev Raymond Heath, Vicar of St Mary's Church, Walmer, is pictured inside the
parish hall in February 1966 with church goers. Warden Mr Cecil Prime
presents Rev Heath with a leaving present of a book signed
by the whole congregation.

69 Spring growth in all its glory frames Deal Borough Council members as they
process from Sunday civic service at St George's Church in May 1962.
Town Sergeant Jock Cowie leads the procession followed by newly
installed Mayor of Deal Ald Norman Cavell, who was in office
again in 1963. Town Clerk Edgar Bradbury and Mayor's
Chaplain, Rev CCG Tufton, follow behind.

Note the contingent of local police forming a guard of honour – more than
the town can boast now. Scouts and Girl Guides line the procession
route and council officials and members of the public look on, many
women wearing hats while young girls are in white ankle socks.
No doubt Basil was in the first floor window of
chemist Stewart Dunn, opposite, to take this photograph.

70 Buglers of the Royal Marines School of Music stand on the balcony of Victoria Memorial Hospital, London Road, Deal on Remembrance Sunday. The Rev John Gore and Matron Stella Grant stand along with members of Deal Borough Council who wait to put their wreaths on the memorial including the Mayor of Deal during 1968 and 1969 Ald John Blake.

71   Staff of Victoria Memorial Hospital, London Road, Deal, pose for Basil in front of the hospital that was built as a tribute to the fallen of the Second World War. Stella Grant, Matron from 1967, stands centre in the front row in the darkest uniform.

In 1943 she had joined the Queen Elizabeth Colonial Nursing Service, travelling to Sierra Leone, Nigeria, Malaya, Singapore and India. To the left of Stella is Sister Crick, Children's ward sister and Mr Faint physiotherapist. On the extreme right is Bill Oram, Porter. To the right of Stella Grant is Sister Smith, Sister of the private wards, alongside her Betty Boditch, Mary Harrison and Evelyn Bates.

Sitting second left is Irene Samuels, then Norma Tucker, Leonora Thompson, Grace Woods, Gwen Oram, and Val Dale. Centre in the back row are Edith Clarke, Richard Whiteside, Nancy Morley and Margaret Crosskerry.

RICEMAN'S FIRE

72 Riceman's was Deal's premier department store, owned by Fred Riceman, and now the site of Boots the Chemist. On Sunday afternoon 6th October, 1963, the alarm was raised as flames and smoke were seen rising from the building.
Here, Basil captures the final moments of the window displays as
the mannequins start to melt.

73 Basil photographs the rear of Riceman's as the fire rages.

74 Palls of black smoke billowing from the burning Riceman's store, photographed by Basil from behind the Black Horse Hotel in Middle Street car park. Local people were hurt and offended when Fred Riceman decided not to rebuild the shop but to concentrate on developing his new Canterbury store.

75 The fire at Riceman's spread rapidly to the other part of the
building in Queen Street, now Iceland's supermarket.

PARTIES, PLAYERS AND PERSONALITIES

76 A birthday party for an unknown group of children photographed by Basil during the 1950s. On the piano are cards for a five year old and the table is laid with glasses for squash and, unusual these days, teacups. As is the case with so many of Basil's photos they reflect the fashions, styles and customs of their day.

77 and 78 Basil really has the Marks and Spencer
staff in party mood as they stand on, and
over, the staircase of The Royal Hotel.

79 Staff of Whispies shoe factory doing the Hokey Cokey at their Christmas party in the Astor Theatre in December 1970. Whispies factory was in Ark Lane, Deal, but closed in 1988 with the loss of 130 jobs.

80 A street party is in full swing in Clifford Gardens, Walmer, to celebrate the Queen's Royal Silver Jubilee in the summer of 1977.

81 Children of Cowdray Square, Mill Hill, Deal, enjoy a street party to celebrate the Royal Silver Jubilee of Queen Elizabeth.

82 Parents and friends look on as children from Southwall Road, Deal, enjoy the
street party to mark the royal anniversary. Also watching are Mayor and
Mayoress of Deal Cllr Stuart 'Oscar' Spears and Mrs Doris Spears.

83 The Guild Players cast of 'Merrie England,' by Edward German and Basil
Hood, pose for a photocall outside the imposing backdrop of Deal castle.
The play was performed on the ramparts during July and August 1965 when
some performances had to be rescheduled because of rain.

Among the cast, standing, are left to right: Louise Scott, Claire Bradshaw, Alec
Thomson, Martin Thomson, Zena Almond, Molly Boyce, Conrad Sherwin, Peter
Eckersley, Iris Doms, Ronald Latham, Adrian Doms, Reuben Atkinson and John
Evans. Front row kneeling: Julian Granville, Doris Cohen, Helga Latham, Jackie
Ward, Phyllis Gray, Barbara Latham and right Diane Almond.

84 'Lover's Leap', by Philip Johnson was performed by the Guild Players in March 1968 at The Globe Theatre in aid of the Friends of Deal Hospital. Left to right: Zena Almond, Doris Cohen, Tony Kilshawe (Director), Glenys Cresswell and John Morris. The Guild Players began as the St George's Church drama group in 1958 at their base, St George's Hall, which was named The Little Theatre. In 1981 it was renamed The Kilshawe Theatre as a tribute and memorial to Tony for his contribution to the players.

85 Although most of Deal Dramatic Society's plays have been staged at the Astor Theatre, 'The Post Horn Gallop', by Derek Benfield, was one of several put on at the Royal Marines Globe Theatre – a reminder of the generosity of the marines with their facilities.

Left to right standing were: Phyllis Gray (Director), two Royal Marine helpers, David Willis, Martin Thomson, Bernie Grivel and Paul Davis. Sitting: Colin Clark, Iris Doms, Judy Wilson, Glenn Swanborough, Rosemary Davis, Dot Abbot and Madelaine Franklin.

86 Members and cast of Deal Dramatic Society pause for a photocall during rehearsals for 'Every Other Evening,' at the Royal Marines Globe Theatre. The comedy, by Francois Campaux and adapted by Jack Popplewell, was in aid of the British Heart Foundation in 1971.

Left to right: John Evans, Norman and Mary Woolfenden, Terence Waldron, Dot Abbot, Iris Doms, Susan Paxman, Roger Brown, Phyllis Gray, Fay Perez from the British Heart Foundation local branch, who also produced the play, and John Rudkin. Sitting in the front are Judy Wilson, left, and Sylvia Fowler.

87 Deal Youth Orchestra performed at the Astor Theatre on Saturday 1st October 1966. The young conductor was David Johnson and among the music the orchestra performed were Hayden's Toy Symphony and three pieces from Gilbert and Sullivan's Yeoman of the Guard. A report on the event noted the orchestra "included a few Royal Marines but all were well within 'the ranks of youth.'"

There was a slight problem and some laughter when a tin of dried peas being used in the percussion section as a rattle lost its lid and showered the orchestra with peas. Choirs also took to the stage and Dover Grammar School For Girls Choir "set the standard for the evening."

88 "Can I lick the bowl?" This picture, taken by Basil in April 1957, underlines the wide variety of events the Astor Theatre has hosted over the decades and the diversity of Basil's assignments.

Here alsatians Maggie and Emma have been photographed as part of the publicity for a leisure exhibition at the Astor Theatre, organised by the Rotary Club. The dogs belonged to Miss Oldacres of the Deal branch of the Sheep, Police and Army Dog Society.

89 One, two, three o'clock rock … around the ballroom, to the Teen and Twenty Club at the Astor Theatre.

90 John Simmons, Entertainments and Publicity Manager for Deal Borough Council, presents a copy of The Beatles second LP, 'With The Beatles,' to 16 year old Diane Niblett for becoming the 10,000th customer of the Teen and Twenty Club during its 26 week run in 1964 at the Astor Theatre.

With Diane are her friends Christine Groombridge and Mary Denton.

91 The Astor Theatre, in Stanhope Road, Deal, holds many memories for local people and hosted a wide variety of events over the decades. Here ballroom dancers step out in style in the early 1960s.

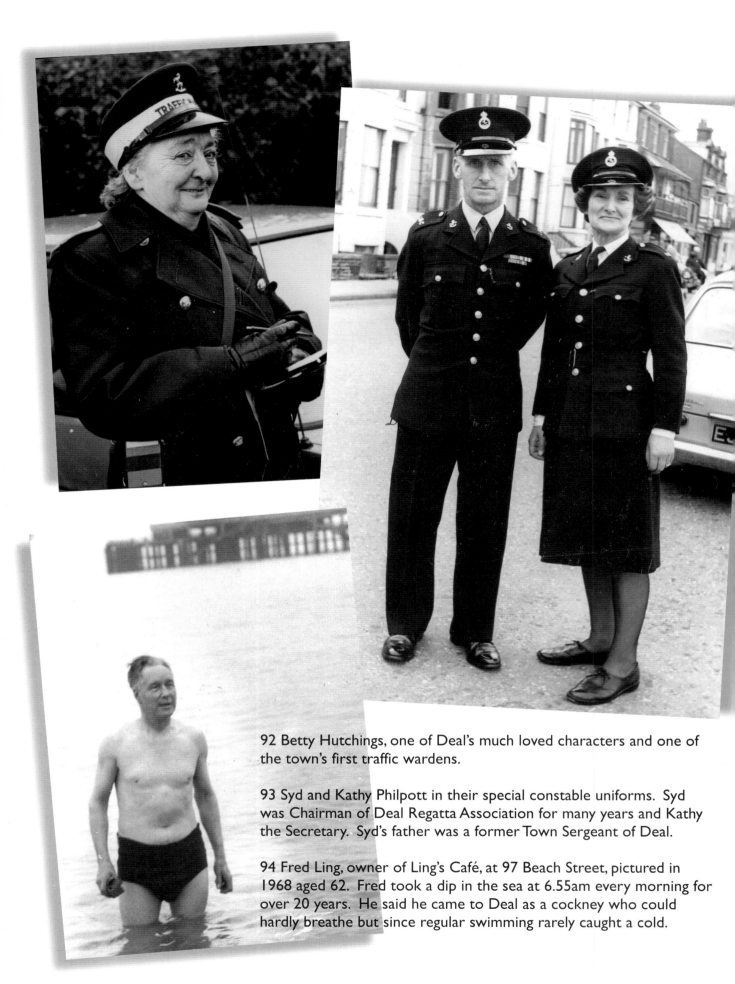

92 Betty Hutchings, one of Deal's much loved characters and one of the town's first traffic wardens.

93 Syd and Kathy Philpott in their special constable uniforms. Syd was Chairman of Deal Regatta Association for many years and Kathy the Secretary. Syd's father was a former Town Sergeant of Deal.

94 Fred Ling, owner of Ling's Café, at 97 Beach Street, pictured in 1968 aged 62. Fred took a dip in the sea at 6.55am every morning for over 20 years. He said he came to Deal as a cockney who could hardly breathe but since regular swimming rarely caught a cold.

95 John Simmons, Entertainments and Publicity Manager for Deal Borough Council in his office in the Timeball Tower, Deal. Above the fireplace – coal fires in winter – is a copy of the front cover of the 1953 Deal Town Guide. Behind John are posters for the Teen and Twenty Club that he began at the Astor Theatre in the early 1960s and a tourism poster imploring 'Make Tracks For Deal'.

BETTESHANGER COLLIERY

96 Many people now ask what coalfield, what mines? But the Kent coalfield pits
of Betteshanger, Tilmanstone, Snowdown and Chislet, near Canterbury, were very
much in the news during Basil's photographic career and he and his camera
recorded the many changes and final demise of the last colliery at
Betteshanger in 1989.

97 Betteshanger Colliery pithead wheel stands as a backdrop to the impressive display of trophies won by the Betteshanger Colliery First Aid Team, including the National Coal Board trophy, in the 1960s. From left to right: Alec Smart, Andy Morrison, Stuart 'Oscar' Spears, Jock Creasey, Con Connolly and Bill Mottershaw.

98 An aerial view of Betteshanger Colliery, now the site of the proposed Betteshanger Business Park. In the centre is the landmark pithead wheel surrounded by colliery buildings and equipment.

99 Dr Alan Calder 'the pit doctor', holding the yardstick presented to him by Betteshanger miners. Dr Calder, who would regularly go down the mine, was also the Walmer lifeboat doctor and practiced at the Balmoral Surgery, in Victoria Road, Deal.

100 The tables are laid ready for a dinner of the Mill Hill OAP branch held at the
Welfare Club, Mill Hill, in the 1970s. On the top table are, left to right,:
unknown, then Phyllis Harrison, Terry Harrison, John Moyle, Joe Burke and
Nora Powell, Chairman of the group.

101 Emanuel Shinwell, later Baron Shinwell, better known as Manny Shinwell, stands centre with, from left, Terry Harrison and Bert Golding and, right, Joe Bell and Nick Richardson, Betteshanger Branch NUM Secretary. Manny Shinwell (1884-1986) was a British trade union official and Labour politician.

102 An older Manny Shinwell with left: Con Sullivan, Joe Bell, and Mo Hudson, second right, and Paddy O'Leary, far right, at the Welfare Club, Mill Hill.

103 Jack Dunn stands beside his portrait, painted by artist Margaret Burlton.
Margaret's parents lived in Walmer and she produced a series of Kent coalfield
paintings, including some sketched at the coalface. Jack was General
Secretary of the Kent National Union of Mineworkers from 1957 to 1980,
previously branch secretary of Betteshanger NUM branch for nine
years and on the National Executive of the NUM.

Jack came to Kent with his family from Bloxwich when he
was about 12 years old and started in Snowdown pit on his 14th
birthday; too short to see over the top of an underground coal tub.
His family returned to the Midlands when he was 17, but he stayed in
Kent at Tilmanstone Colliery. Jack Dunn moved to Betteshanger Colliery
in 1946 and was elected branch secretary two years later. He died in 2002.

104 Betteshanger Brass Band members stand for Basil in their smart uniforms in this photograph taken in the 1980s. The band was formed in 1932 by miner George Gibb and his colleagues as a form of relaxation after their days' toil underground. Now in the process of reverting to its original name of Betteshanger Colliery Band, it is based at the Betteshanger Social Welfare Sports Club, Mill Hill, and plays a number of indoor and outdoor concerts throughout the year.

Left to right back row: third from left Michael Brimson, Nigel Bogue, Unknown, Denis Atkinson, Alan Adshead, Martin Dickerson, Kathleen Harvey, Sue Holland (nee Thomas). Middle row: Ian Thomas, Mark Ashley, Bill Pugh, Steve Grindrod, Nicola Southwick, Steve Wright, Kim Harvey, Doug Walker, Unknown, unknown, Mick Easterbrook and Alan Langley. Front row: John Harvey, Dave Burridge, Joe Baggs, Professor Walter Hargreaves, Alan Finemore, Roger Morgan-Williams and Ivor Thomas.

105-110 The moment Betteshanger miners, their families and supporters had been dreading and one which changed the local landscape forever. Basil captures a frame by frame record of the Betteshanger Colliery pithead wheel being toppled after the closure of the pit in 1989, just a year short of the centenary of the discovery of coal in Kent.

SCHOOLS, SCOUTS AND BROWNIES

111 Lower Walmer School pupils gather together for their final nativity play
photographed in December 1969. The school, in Canada Road, Walmer,
closed in 1970 and is now the site of Wolfe Court,
on the corner of Campbell Road.

Basil was so well known in the district even local children would recognise him.
He recorded in his notebook, with obvious pride, that on a visit to
one school the children all called out "It's Basil!"

112 Walmer Secondary School pupils in good spirits at the start of their charity
walk on Sunday 30th March 1968 to raise money for Shelter. Ald Alistair
Lawton, former Mayor of Deal and Chairman of Kent County Council
Education Committee, saw the pupils off during brilliant sunshine.

Between them, the pupils covered 2,700 miles via Betteshanger, Tilmanstone,
Eythorne, Whitfield, Langdon and Martin. Deal Beach Parlours, Pilcher &
Chittenden greengrocers and Sharpe's Dairy provided refreshments.

113 St Ethelburga's Convent School was in Queen Street, Deal, now the site of
Somerfield and Co-op supermarket, and closed around 1970. Staff and
former pupils of the school, a few in their distinctive summer boaters,
held their first reunion at the Royal Hotel on 27th August 1988 and
are pictured alongside the hotel at the top of Oak Street.

114 John Brown, much loved caretaker and lollipop man of Deal Parochial School, when it was based in its original site of London Road, Deal, poses with pupils on his retirement in 1989 after 25 years service with the school.

115 Deal Secondary School for Boys pupils, packed lunches at the ready, gather outside Deal railway station before heading off for a day trip to London with a boat ride on the Thames and a visit to Heathrow Airport around 1965.

116 No prizes for guessing the theme of this Brownie get together in June 1964.
Mad Hatters, Cheshire cats and March Hares along with other characters from
Alice in Wonderland pose for Basil at their Brownie Revels at Hawkshill Camp,
Kingsdown. Seven Packs from Deal and Walmer district took part and the
winners of the fancy dress competition were 1st Deal (Depot) pack.

117 Scout Master Harold Mercer is presented with the Golden Acorn award for
long service by District Commissioner Godfrey Davis watched by
youngsters from the 2nd Deal (Walmer) Sea Scouts.
Basil took the photograph in the late 1960s or early 1970s in the group
headquarters in Marine Road Walmer. On the right is Chairman of the group
Sydney Cox and on the left Secretary Len Spain.

THE ROYAL MARINES

118 Basil photographed the King's Squad performing their drill display as part of the Royal Marines Centenary Parade and events in 1961, and by doing so captured the buildings along Beach Street, at the top of King Street, in the background including The Lobster Pot Café and Divito's Ice Cream Parlour.

119 Columns of Royal Marines set out on parade from their depot in Canada Road as generations had done before them. They pass the Marine Café which later became Jeff's Tattoo Parlour. Jeff died in 2009 and no doubt tattooed quite a few marines during his career.

Basil probably took the photograph from the first floor of 1 The Beach, Walmer, the former National Provincial Bank, a strategic position he used on many occasions.

120 Walmer Castle impressively lit for a performance by the Royal Marines School of Music as part of their centenary celebrations.

121 Lt Col Sir Vivian Dunn, KCVO, OBE, FRAM stands on the stage of the
concert hall at the Depot Royal Marines in Canada Road, Deal, during
one of the many concerts held over the decades.

Lt Col Dunn's career in the Royal Marines spanned 38 years, 15 as Principal
Director of Music at Deal. He retired in 1968 having been a
prolific composer and made many recordings.

122 An impressive floodlit scene photographed by Basil at the Royal Marines
Depot during the dress rehearsal for the Searchlight Tattoo, which opened
in the North Barracks on Thursday 28th July 1960. The tattoo ran until
the following Wednesday with more 9,000 advance ticket sales.

123 The tables are set and the beers are ready in the Sergeants' Mess for just one of the many events Basil photographed there and, no doubt, joined in.

124 The Director of WRENS, Commandant Jean Davies OBE, inspects women on parade at the Depot Royal Marines. Also in the picture is the Commanding Officer Col Jones RM and Third Officer SJ Hogg.

125 The Royal Marines Depot Church of St Michael and All Angels was well known to Basil who had been a choirboy there. The church is photographed by him ready for harvest festival.

Lord George Hamilton, Captain of Deal Castle and former First Lord of the Admiralty, laid the foundation stone for the church in 1905. The church was consecrated in January 1907 and replaced the smaller Chapel School that had been built in 1858.

126 and 127 The Depot Church hosted the weddings of many Royal Marines and their families. Here Lt Martin Garrod and his bride Jill Parks-Smith emerge from the traditional archway of swords formed by fellow officers following their wedding on 1st June 1963.

Inset, a gust of wind gave the bride a little difficulty with her veil. Lt Garrod rose to be Commandant General Royal Marines and as Lt General Sir Martin Garrod was central to peacekeeping in the Balkans in the 1990s. From 1991 Sir Martin was a Deputy Lieutenant for Kent until his death in 2009 aged 73. Lady Garrod, daughter and grandaughter of Royal Marines officers, lives in Walmer.

128 The yearly Royal Marines pantomime was an annual tradition and treat for
the marines' families and hundreds of local people. The first was performed at
the Walmer barracks in 1948 and the last, 'Aladdin and his Lump,' in 1995.
Like so many performances they were held at the Depot's Globe Theatre,
built around 1900 and sadly demolished a few years ago.

This is one of the obligatory annual photographs taken each year by Basil of the
Royal Marines' pantomime Corps de Ballet – service issue boots and all.

129 The first ever production of the Royal Marines Operatic Society was Gilbert and Sullivan's Yeoman of the Guard. It was performed at the Globe Theatre in April 1970. The musical director was John Wheatley, producer Terry Williams, and stage manager Stan Glasspoll. Basil's wife Eve was among the cast.

130 Christmas time and the stirring of the Christmas pudding in the main galley
– another tradition captured by Basil over the years.

131 Lt Col Graham Hoskins OBE MVO FRAM, Principal Director of Music from
1982 to 1989, gallantly conducts to the last aboard an unusual rostrum!
This was the traditional wheeling out ceremony upon retirement
of the Director. Pictured left is Col Richard Dixon,
Commandant, and musicians of the staff band.

132 The opening ceremony of the Centenary Gates at the South Barracks which were presented by the town of Deal in 1961. To the left was Rev Raymond Heath, in uniform Col FC Barton, Lt Col HG Jones, Lt Col Sir Vivian Dunn, KCVO, OBE, FRAM, Mr E Bradbury, Deal Town Clerk (wearing raincoat), and, wearing his Mayoral chain, Captain EH Hopkinson.

133 A very different view of the South Barrack Gates in 1989 laid with floral tributes to the bandsmen killed by an IRA bomb. Prime Minister Margaret Thatcher looks at the tributes with Sir Martin Garrod, Commandant General.

134 Some of the All Stars Band photographed practicing for a concert. The band
was formed by retired Royal Marines musicians, including Basil,
in 1990 as a direct result of the barracks bombing.

They raised money for the disaster fund subsequently set up for what was
planned as a one-off performance but is now an annual event with
much of the proceeds going to the Royal Marines Band
Benevolent Fund and the Deal Memorial Bandstand.

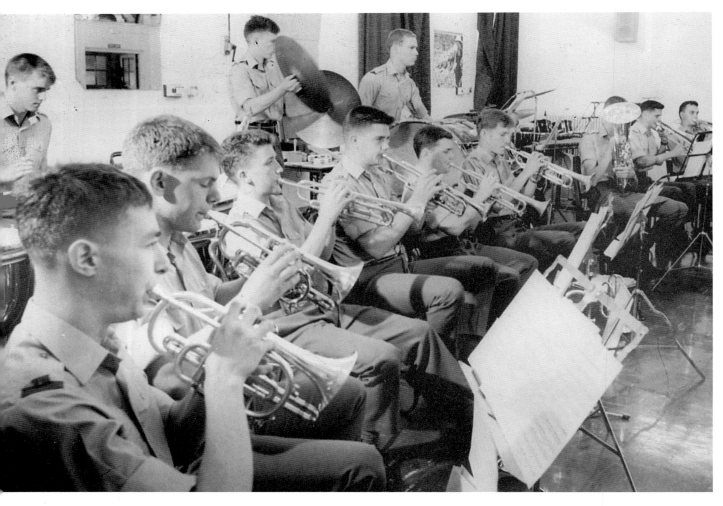

135 This is the photograph Basil took of Royal Marines bandsmen resuming practice soon after IRA terrorists bombed their barracks on 12 September 1989.
The attack killed 11 musicians and injured many more.

The photograph appeared a few days later on the front page of the East Kent Mercury under the headline 'TUNES OF GLORY – Defiant bandsmen play on.'

136 Basil pictured with that issue of the Mercury which carried his photo of the marines practicing.

137 Perhaps Basil Kidd's signature photograph and certainly one of his most impressive. Columns of Royal Marines parade back to barracks along The Strand, Walmer.

ROYALTY AND CELEBRITIES

Huge crowds awaited Princess Diana when she came to the Deal Centre for the Retired in Park Street on 12 September 1989.

Princess Diana performed the opening ceremony for the new centre's shop which had been built with funds from a legacy left by the late Daphne Theobald, local resident and artist.

138 left: Princess Diana is presented with flowers by local children while her plain-clothed detective, senior police officer and crowds look on.

139 below: A marquee was set up in the car park where Princess Diana met more guests at the event.

140-142 More of Basil's photographs of Princess Diana as she greets the crowds at Deal Centre for the Retired in Park Street, dressed in a bright pink suit.

With her in suit and tie was Inspector Ken Wharf, her Personal Protection Officer who grew up in Canterbury.

143 The Queen Mother stands on the dais during her visit to the Depot Royal Marines on 23 May 1956 to open a new accommodation block in the North Barracks. This was an auspicious early diary date for Basil which would be followed the next year with the visit of the Duke of Edinburgh to open the new pier.

144 Basil first photographed the Queen Mother in 1953 on HMS Vanguard at the Spithead Review while he was still a photographer and Bandsman in the Royal Marines. Here, he photographs the Queen Mother during her visit to Deal in 1956.

Basil would photograph the Queen Mother and all the leading members of the Royal family during his career including the Queen. He noted in his diary "Queen Mum best royal for pictures."

145   Girl Guides line the entrance to St Mary's Church, Walmer, as the Queen
Mother leaves Sunday service during one of her many successful stays at
Walmer Castle as Lord Warden of the Cinque Ports.
To her left, the Rev Bruce Hawkins looks on.

146 Comedian and actor Norman Wisdom on Deal beach in 1967 with his
14 year old son Nicholas. Norman lived in Deal from an early age and
became an errand boy for Lipton's, High Street shop. He decided
on a career in showbiz after appearing on the stage during his
Second World War service. Although Norman Wisdom
became famous he returned to Deal regularly and
in later life became Patron of the local
Talking Newspaper for the Blind.

147 At first glance Basil had travelled to Cornwall to photograph the actors and
comedians Ronnie Barker and Ronnie Corbett. But the BBC production team
transformed part of Coppin Street in Deal, including mock
cobblestones, to film one of 'The Two Ronnies' sketches
in August 1973, watched by many locals.

148 David Frost and Harold Wilson pose for Basil outside the Zetland Arms, Kingsdown, in September 1977. They had stopped for lunch at the pub during a break in filming at Walmer Castle.

They were working on a TV series for Yorkshire Television called 'A Prime Minister on Prime Ministers' and were filming William Pitt's role as Lord Warden of the Cinque Ports which was conferred on him by King George III in 1792.

Speaking at the time Harold Wilson said he was aware of "Pitt's deep love for Walmer Castle."

149 Basil recalled in his notebook that as a freelance photographer he did a lot of work for the Dover ferry companies. On one occasion he was asked to photograph a famous pop star who would be travelling on the Pride of Dover.

"Turned out to be Michael Jackson. Didn't know him. Called him Malcolm by mistake," Basil recalled in his notebook. But he got his autograph. The said Malcolm is pictured here talking to ferry Captain Pat Hambrook.

ALL IN A DAY'S WORK

The photos on the next few pages highlight the wide variety of photographs Basil took over 40 years. At the time they simply illustrated the news in the East Kent Mercury or were requested by local organisations. Now they act as an historical record – but for Basil they were all in a day's work.

150 Basil's photographs from May 1959 capture a train crash at Walmer station when only the quick thinking of a signalman averted 'a serious disaster' and potential deaths. Railway maintenance men who were working overnight laying tracks for electrification of the line near Martin Mill, uncoupled five trucks that held 500 tons of rails.

151 But the trucks ran out of control down the 1 in 70 slope into Walmer station. Luckily, 24 year old signalman Gerry Hutchings, from Mongeham Road, diverted the trucks into a nearby siding. They still smashed through the buffers, tore themselves to pieces and crashed back on to the line. If not diverted they could have crashed on to houses in Telegraph Road causing, at least, serious injury.

152 Deal Telephone Exchange staff are pictured in February 1961 in the old
building in Stanhope Road that had opened in 1929. This
became the offices of accountants Reeves and Neylan
and is currently used by Creative Partnerships.

The staff are standing with the exchange behind them on the first floor of the
building at the leaving do for Marjorie Sims (seated) who emigrated to New
Zealand. Left to right: Joan Saunders, Barbara Kember, Kitt Ablett, Margaret
Powell, Marie Senior, Margaret Bartram, Barbara Cox, Margaret Oliver,
Margaret Coomby, Patricia Mendham, Elaine Siviter and Chris Mendham.

Deal exchange moved to new premises in West Street, at a cost of £160,000, and
on 16 January 1969 the new automated service began at 1.32pm.

153 Members of Deal Volunteer Emergency Service stand ready with their
motorbikes for deliveries in April 1964, standing in Blenheim Road,
near Douglas Terrace.

On the left is Richard Clements with his two stroke Ariel Arrow. Richard
had read about the service, set up in Surrey by Margaret Ryerson in
February 1962, to deliver vaccines during a smallpox outbreak.

Richard enlisted his friends and in their first days in service went to the rescue
of ambulancemen who had been called to help an injured girl. The volunteers
guided the ambulance over sandhills in thick fog.

With Richard are, from left, Ron Lancaster, Fred Fisher,
Tony Hammond, Bob Pickard, Tom Burke and area organiser Peter Richards.

154 Ald John Blake, Mayor of Deal in 1968 and 1969, is shown how a Linotype machine works by John Ford at the East Kent Mercury printing works in Queen Street, Deal while Editor Richard Jenkins looks on.

The lead based 'hot metal' typesetting machines were used until photocomposition systems were introduced at the works, situated behind the Mercury offices on land that is now a doctors' surgery.

155 Wrapped up from the cold and ready for a day out, are staff, friends and family of Marks and Spencer, Deal. They pose with the driver of the East Kent Road Car Company bus in Stanley Road at the side of the Victoria Road Baptist Church. The picture was taken around 1956.

156 The most surreal of Basil's photographs, an advertising picture for the sale of nuclear fallout shelters as sold by Arthur Letheren, local builder.

The picture appeared in the East Kent Mercury in March 1962 and promoted the 'exhibition site' at the junction of Middle Street and Oak Street that is now a car park. The site was formerly the Royal Oak public house and the shelter seems to be in the cellar area.

Opposite is Scarden's fish and chip shop. This picture, in which there is a glimpse of three people standing inside the shelter, seems strange if not comical now but reflects the very real concerns about nuclear threats at the time.

157 One week to go before the 1983 General Election and Prime Minister Margaret Thatcher waves goodbye to Conservative party members after a flying visit to their HQ in Deal High Street before going on to Dover in her campaign bus.

She ignores the national media scrum and protestors with their banners. To the left, an enterprising representative of Oak Street Market, now a restaurant opposite the Town Hall, gets in on the act brandishing his advertising placard!

DEAL REGATTA AND CARNIVAL 1960S STYLE

158 Regatta night 1962 at the Astor Theatre and Deal Regatta Queen, Carol Smith, extreme right, poses for Basil along with the visiting Regatta Queens. The band for the night watches from the stage behind.

159 Deal Regatta Queen Carolyn Pack with her attendants Christine Rigden and Anne Jackson, right, on their carnival float in 1967.

160 Actor Geoffrey Adams, who played 'Laudie' in Dixon of Dock Green, crowns the 1965 Deal Regatta Queen Primrose Arnold at the Astor Theatre. Attendants Beryl Carveth, left, and Christine Thomas, right are pictured with Primrose.

161 The 1969 Regatta Court with Regatta Queen Jennifer Riley, centre, and attendants Margaret Reece, right, and Yvonne Almond, left.

162 Deal and District Girl Pipers and Dancers are pictured performing in front of the Zetland Arms at Kingsdown during Deal Regatta Week, an annual engagement for them. The band was a traditional and familiar part of the carnival procession and at a wide variety of functions in the district.

Campbell Thompson formed the Deal Girl Pipe Band in 1955. He came up with the idea and advertised in the local paper for girls of 10 to 12 years old who might be interested in joining.

He had enough response to start classes and a committee was formed of the girls' parents to help raise money for uniforms and equipment. William Adamson and his wife later took over the running of the band which finally folded in the 1990s.

163 Zena Almond, of Zena's Florist, West Street, entered an annual float during
the 1960s. Zena, on board 'An Olde English Garden', is pictured
with floral wishing well while slightly behind to her right, in a
bonnet, is her niece Diane Almond.

164 For many years the Hilson family, of Gladstone Road, Walmer, entered the carnival parade. Here, with the theme of Fantails for 1963, are Lew Hilson, in top hat, with his wife Kath and their young daughter Janet and son John.

In the foreground is their friend Eleanor Boothby, of Boothby's butcher's shop on The Strand, Walmer.

165 An entry to the Deal Carnival by staff of Baldwin's department store which was in Deal High Street, on the corner of Market Street. The store later became Laughton's before closure in 2009.

Each year Baldwin's staff chose a theme around their suppliers. The theme for the year of this photograph, at the end of the 1950s, was wool as portrayed by women of the French Revolution knitting below a guillotine. The younger girl on the float is Elizabeth Barber, daughter of the Manager of Baldwin's, Wilfred Barber. One of the male assistants looks dapper modelling the store's formal hire wear.

166 Another annual entrant to the carnival was Graham Hunter Fashions of 17 The Strand, Walmer. The shop was opposite the lifeboat station and was run by Mary Hardy. Basil has photographed the float at the Royal Marines Barracks where the carnival used to assemble before the procession began. Later, Basil would stand at the window of his studio and home at 32 Victoria Road and photograph the parade as it passed by.

THIS SPORTING LIFE

167 Betteshanger Rugby Club squad for the 1960-61 season pictured left to right: Charlie Ricketts, John Ace, John Crann, Gerald Griffiths, Keith Whitehall, Derek Evans, Charlie Burbinster, Jack Golding, Mick Jailler, Glyn Ashton, John Whiteside, Ray Dale, Dia Collins, Len Court and Harry Tonks.

Front row: Tim Bradbury, Ray Reese, Cliff Cowens, Mick Streeting, Bob Spain, Geoff Mockridge, Glyn Higgins and John Nightengale.

168 And there's another lot in the wash – Thelma Davies, known to many as 'Ma' hangs out some of the five teams worth of Betteshanger rugby shirts she washed and repaired every week at her home in Cavell Square, Mill Hill. The kits were dried around the house and in front of the coal fire in the living room.

Mrs Davies also washed Betteshanger football club strips as well as family washing for husband 'Bingo' who worked at Betteshanger Colliery.

169 A great action shot by Basil shows Graham Robinson, fly-half for Betteshanger
Rugby Club being tackled by the opposition during a match in the 1970s.

170 An informal shot taken by Basil of Deal Wanderers Rugby Club team v Hanover University during their tour in 1973 or 1974. Deal Wanderers, in the hooped strip, are, from back left to right: Derek Pickford, Vic Pidduck, Dave Hinchcliffe, John Wilde, Dave Pinkney, Darrel Chaffey, Ray Sipek, Mick Davis, Paul Mount and Dave Rose. Front left to right: Ray Taylor, Alec Marsh, Pete Davenport, Ian Storer and Rus Waddon.

DEAL WANDERERS SPORTS CLUB
RUGBY "A" XV 1963/64

BASIL M. KIDD, Deal

B. Peace   J. Woolmore   A. Queen   D. Thompson   V. Twyman   G. McMallan   M. Elliott   A. Carney   R. Green
R. Graham   R. Philpott   V. Lewis   D. Rose   A. Bennett   A. Marsh   K. Ashington

171 Those were the days my friend. Deal Wanderers Rugby Club 'A' XV of the
1963/4 season, framed and mounted for posterity.

172 Deal Town football team of around 1958 pictured in front of the club house at the Charles ground. Pictured left to right back are thought to be manager Jim Buist, John Sutton, Ron Margeson, Dave Henworth, Eric Smith, Dick Bartley, physio, Bill Howett, unknown and possibly Darkie Edwards.

Front left to right, Mr Kelly, Gordon Killip, Jock Parker, Roy Hillier, Fred Lillicrap and Fred Galvin.

173 Members of the Deal and District Girl Pipers form a line up for the football club's manager's and showbiz game at the Charles ground in February 1961. The old club buildings are behind them.

174 'Like your necklace.' Chart topping singer Tommy Steele, third from left, with England player Billie Wright and other showbiz team members, admire the ceremonial chain of Mayor Norman Cavell during the Showbix XI v Manager's XI charity game at Deal Town on Sunday 19th February 1961. The club team lost 3-1 but raised more than £300 for local charities. Police tried to keep order among the hundreds of spectators – 'mostly gaily dressed girls'.

A few fans wrote their names on a Jaguar car they presumed was Tommy's but his motor was parked in Lees Road! Ten minutes before full time, Tommy was carried off with a 'hurt ankle' but then nipped smartly over back fences, allotments and through the back door of Deal Town trainer Ernie Wallace's home where he had a cup of tea and then sped off, avoiding the crowds.

175 The 1964 season winners pose for their annual photograph for Basil outside Deal Rowing Club headquarters on The Marina. Included in the back row left to right are: E Vallance, A Marsh, B Gray, V Twyman, A Queen.

Standing from left to right are: C Bell, J Niblett, R Goldfinch, J Terry, R Mead, G Dadd, C Boughton, A Hook, P Epps, D Dadd, E Swatton, P Sanders, B Dadd, P Dadd, R Goldfinch, A Philpott, R Hibbert, D Latham, P Combes, R Whiteside, R Steer, B Peace, P Harrison, J Whiteside, F Roberts, D Goodban, N Barrs, F Fuggle, G Bell, A Card, J Bailey, J Tyer, R Philpott, R Wybourne, F Card, A Card and B Harris.

In the front are: B Hook coxwain, T Hook and P Card, Coxwain. The impressive haul of silverware included the Coastal Amateur Rowing Association (CARA) grand aggregate, senior fours champions, junior/senior fours champions, junior fours champions, novice fours champions, junior pairs fours champions, south coast senior fours champions and Bideford bowl.

176 It's a family affair. Basil photographed the Card family and relatives who
were all members of Deal Rowing Club. Left is young Marie Card, cox and
daughter of Peter Card. Alongside are Peter's brothers Frank and Alex. Next are
brothers-in-law Peter Card and Jack Twyman, and Alex's son Julian.

177 With golden locks flowing, Deal Rowing Club junior-senior fours are photographed by Basil as he stands on Deal pier to capture the scene during the annual rowing regatta in 1974.

In the bow of the boat is Micky Foster, then Freddy Roberts Junior, Larry Smith, Alec Gilchrist and coxwain Steve Mercer.

The crew won the race but strokeman Alec rowed part of it with a broken seat and later needed a quick hospital visit to sort out the resulting injury.

178 David Ennals, MP for Dover and Deal, christens two new Deal Rowing Club
boats at a double naming ceremony in front of Deal pier entrance in June 1968,
watched by members and friends of the club. Pete Sanders, club Captain,
stands to the right of David Ennals alongside the fours boat named after him.

Jim Bailey, past Vice Captain, stands next to the new pairs boat named after him.
In the background is part of the old Quarterdeck building adjacent to the
Antwerp Hotel, now The Bohemian. After the naming ceremony
David Ennals rowed with some of the senior fours in the new boat.

179 President of Deal Bowling Club, Major W McKerrow, sends down the first wood of the season on Saturday 27th April 1968 at the club in Mill Road.

180 Right: Victoria Park Bowling Club ladies pose for Basil after winning the Kent County Women's Bowling Association Mollie Cleggett Memorial Trophy in 1989. Left to right back: Judith Cullen, Shirley Lawrence, Doris Thompson, Eileen Pidduck and Thelma Clemmey. Left to right front: Jouhie Bawden, Frances Parker, Liz Coley, Marian Addison and Ruth Coleman.

ACKNOWLEDGEMENTS

I am indebted to Nick Kidd, son of Basil, who generously offered me the opportunity of using his father's extensive archive for this book.

Many thanks to my partner Charles Finn for all his continued help and support.

I would like to thank the following people for their help: Richard Ablett, Margaret Adamson, Paul Amos, Bill and Sue Ashby, Nick Atkins, Vicky Barnsley, Terry Birkett, Olga Calder, Tony Cheeseman, Julie Chmura, Les Coe, Doris Cohen, Con Connolly, Rose Connolly, Judith Cullen, Bert and Georgina Curling, Duncan Currie, Jim Davies, Nickie and Clifford Davies, Maggie Dunn, Brian and Sue Foy, Lady Garrod, Steve Glover, Mr and Mrs L Hilson and John Hilson, Cynthia Horncastle, Anne Marie Howden, Sir Wayne King, David Latham, Sheila Latham, Carol Lenthall, Julie Limbrick, Sylvia Main, Pat Mendham, Allan Mercer, Pete and Val Mercer, Lorraine Mewson, Steven Milne, Stephen Misson ARMC, Jean Moore, Margaret Moulson, Malcolm Norman, Arthur Parrett, Robert Peace, Michael Rogers, Dave and Margaret Rose, Marie Senior, Doreen Turner. Jill Watson and Judy Wilson.

I also express my appreciation to the following individuals and organisations for their assistance: Natalie Barnes, Assistant Town Clerk, Deal Town Council; Sue Briggs, Chief Reporter, East Kent Mercury; Deal Library staff; Steve Griffiths and Betteshanger Brass Band; Peter Jull and staff of Zoom Photos, Deal, and Graham Smith, Editor, East Kent Mercury,

Once again, I would like to thank my publisher Nick Evans of Bygone Publishing for all his hard work in producing this book.

BIBLIOGRAPHY

East Kent Mercury various editions

Laker, John (1921) History of Deal. 2nd edn. Deal: TF Pain and Sons

Lane, Andrew (2000) Royal Marines Deal, a pictorial history. Tiverton: Halsgrove.